BECOME A LEADER IN YOUR INDUSTRY USING SOCIAL MEDIA

JEAN PAUL PAULYNICE, MBA

Published by Paulynice Consulting Group, LLC

ISBN: 978-1-7330427-3-4 (Paperback)
ISBN: 978-1-7330427-4-1 (eBook)
ISBN: 978-1-7330427-5-8 (Hardback)

Printed in the United States of America.

CONTENTS

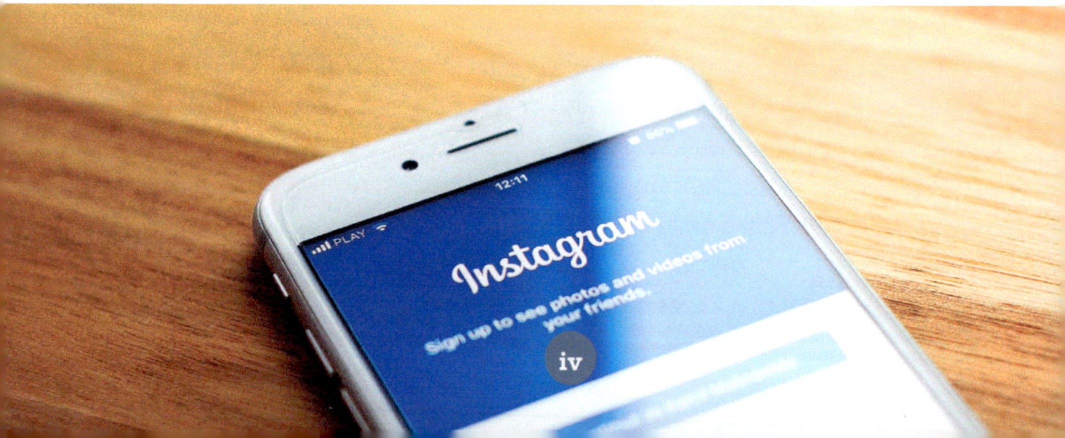
12:11
Instagram
Sign up to see photos and videos from your friends.

THE POWER OF SOCIAL MEDIA

Introduction

Social media is flourishing. According to a global digital report by We Are Social, 4.38 billion people out of a total 7.67 billion global population are internet users. Out of this number, there are 3.48 billion active social media users. It is estimated that the average internet user now spends around six hours on the internet each day, mostly using mobile devices. It is clear that social media is a big part of our society and our lives. Even if you're not a fan of social media, it is impossible to ignore its significance to connect brands and customers.

Successful brands know that social media participation is no longer an option, but a requirement. Some years ago, many small businesses had a minimal online presence if any. In fact, I remember talking to one small business owner a while back about the need of having a website, and he shook his head and told me that his business didn't really need it. He explained that it was too expensive and time consuming to build and to run. And that most of their clients would never have to search them online.

It's fascinating how things have since changed. Consumers have become more empowered and are demanding more from businesses. Unlike those halcyon days, consumers are more aware of the power of social media. And so is your competition.

Clients and customers will talk about you whether you have an online presence or not. People will still look up your business for reviews before contacting you or visiting your storefront or restaurant.

Don't you want to know what those reviews say? Wouldn't you like to be able to do some damage control when things don't work as planned? Don't you want to be able to defend your business in case of a murky public slag? Don't you want to build a positive online reputation?

Obviously, we all want that. We want to be in control of the narrative. We want to create a strong brand that is firmly founded on values and superseded by good reputation. Social media gives you this power – to listen and to engage your customers directly, wherever they are in the world.

Social media will allow you to catch the attention of new prospects and engage with new leads. No matter the size of your company or business, you can actively use social media to start conversations with your target market and elevate your brand.

From my experience as a small business owner who has successfully implemented strong social media campaigns that drive traffic, enhance visibility, and build active communities, I know how important social media is. Surprisingly, I have also seen how much our competitors charge to implement these same efforts (they're quite expensive!), making it almost impossible for small businesses to access these services.

It's for that single reason why I decided to open a business to help small business owners grow their brands and protect their bottom lines. Paulynice Consulting Group provides top-notch services at a fraction of what others are charging, allowing your business to leverage the immense power of social media.

I want to share my insights with you on how I've used social media to scale my brand and to reach a more extensive market. We have developed a robust A-Z approach, which small businesses can implement for social media strategies that yield a massive return on investment. This eBook is your ultimate guide to how you can leverage social media for your business' success.

Let's get started, folks.

1

CHAPTER

WHY SHOULD YOU CONSIDER USING SOCIAL MEDIA?

As a small business owner, your biggest goal and priority should be to gain fast, effective, and sustainable online traction. It is, therefore, best to set your social media efforts around the most popular social media channels where you can follow proven lead-generation strategies and generate consistent return on investment. Importantly, your choice of social media network should depend on three significant factors:

1. Where are your customers most concentrated?
2. Where is your audience most accessible?
3. Where will your audience most actively engage with your content and ads?

Let's look at some of the ways you can use social media platforms like Facebook and Twitter to ace your game. But before we get there, is social media really worth the salt? The answer is a resounding YES. And here is why:

- There is a large number of people to be reached at the same time;

- Social media as a platform is becoming bigger and more defined;
- People are beginning to understand and accept social media as part of their lives;
- In most instances, little effort is required to kick-start a worthwhile lead-generating scheme;
- Social media is here to stay; hence, it can be relied on as a platform.

SOCIAL MEDIA OPPORTUNITIES AND CHALLENGES

How Can Social Media Empower/ Influence Your Small Business?

The advent and spread of social media changed the course of human interaction all over the world. The revolution has also swept the business front and changed the way businesses interact with their consumers. Digital marketing plays a crucial role in building a brand and increasing its visibility. Let's look at some of the ways social media marketing can empower your small business.

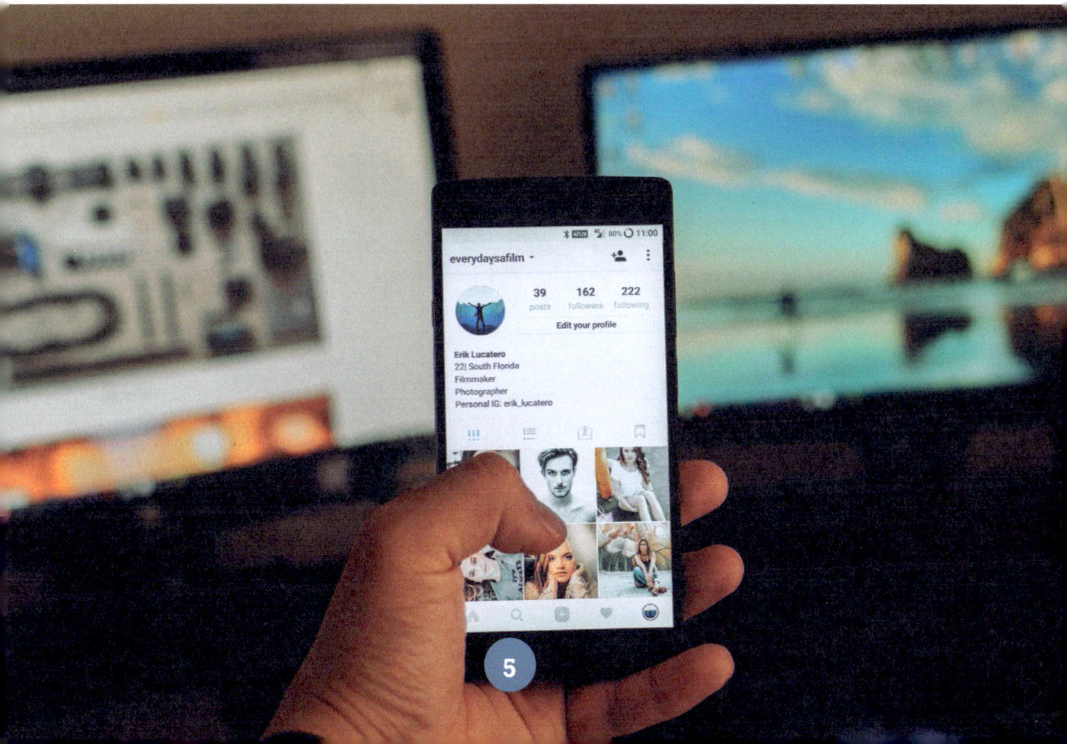

1 Enhanced Visibility

Social media platforms provide an opportunity to get your products and services noticed by a broader market. With the correct marketing strategy, you can get consumers to visit your website and subsequently buy your products. With over 2.38 billion active users monthly, Facebook, for instance, can provide an excellent untapped market for your business.

2 Build Your Brand's Awareness

Studies have revealed that 33% of customers use social media to get information on new products and services. You can leverage on this to stamp your authority in your niche by showing your expertise to your consumers through social media. This will build a strong reputation for your brand to your potential customers.

3 Increased Interaction with Your Customers

Your business can now connect much easier with your customers through social media. They can relay their opinions, reviews, and complaints about your products and services directly. You can engage with these customers instantaneously and on the fly. You have the opportunity to respond promptly, build your rapport, and encourage constant communication.

4 Cost-Effective Marketing

Sales and marketing are considered essential aspects of any business. Traditional marketing is very costly, and businesses spend quite a lot on it. Social media marketing is cheaper than the conventional outbound strategies, such as cold calling, printed leaflets, and TV and magazine advertisements. You can opt to market your products for free on social media to those who are already following you or your business. If you choose to pay for your advertisement, you can expand your audience and target specific groups to maximize the returns.

5 Your Business Gets Competitive Advantage

By embracing the most effective marketing strategy, your business will soar above its competition. Your competition might be using its social media wrong. You can capitalize on this to get more clients familiar with your products and services. You can also use social media to offer excellent customer service, respond to your customer inquiries, and market your business to endear your customers.

6 Build Customer Loyalty

Research shows that over 70% of customers would refer a brand to others merely because they received a prompt response on social media. Customers will feel more appreciated by constant feedback and will become more loyal to your brand.

7 Get Your Customers' Perspectives

Your business gets the chance to understand your customers' tastes and preferences through interactions with them. You can use this to improve your products and services and even tailor them to the customers' preferences. Your customers will feel valued and appreciated. You can also use the interaction to understand your target audience and discover an untapped market.

8 Higher Conversion Rates

Digital interaction gives your business the opportunity to convert itself to a more human-like venture that people can easily relate with. Your customers will want to be associated with your business if you listen to them, give them relevant content, and portray a positive image of your brand. This will result in more social sharing and increased conversion rates.

Social Media Risks and Challenges for Small Business Owners

As already established above, social media can be a potent tool for your business. However, it is essential to fully consider all its benefits and risks before settling on the most suitable approach for your business.

• Damaged Reputation

Social media presence comes with the risk of ruining your businesses reputation. If you do not address the concerns raised by your clients or mishandle their comments, they can quickly spread negative feedback, which will affect your brand's image. Your brand's reputation can also be affected by negative comments that may be raised by your competition on social media.

• Additional Expenses

Your small business will incur extra expenses in a bid to be more active on social media. You may be required to hire professionals to manage the pages or spend money on acquiring in-house talent. You may also have to pay for advertising if you opt for a paid ad. Creation of content will also require extra funds, for example, the cost of making videos or having professional photos taken.

• Reduce Time Wasted

Since social media requires regular monitoring, it may end up consuming much of your productive time. Your followers may demand timely responses to their comments and may interpret a delay as not being valued enough.

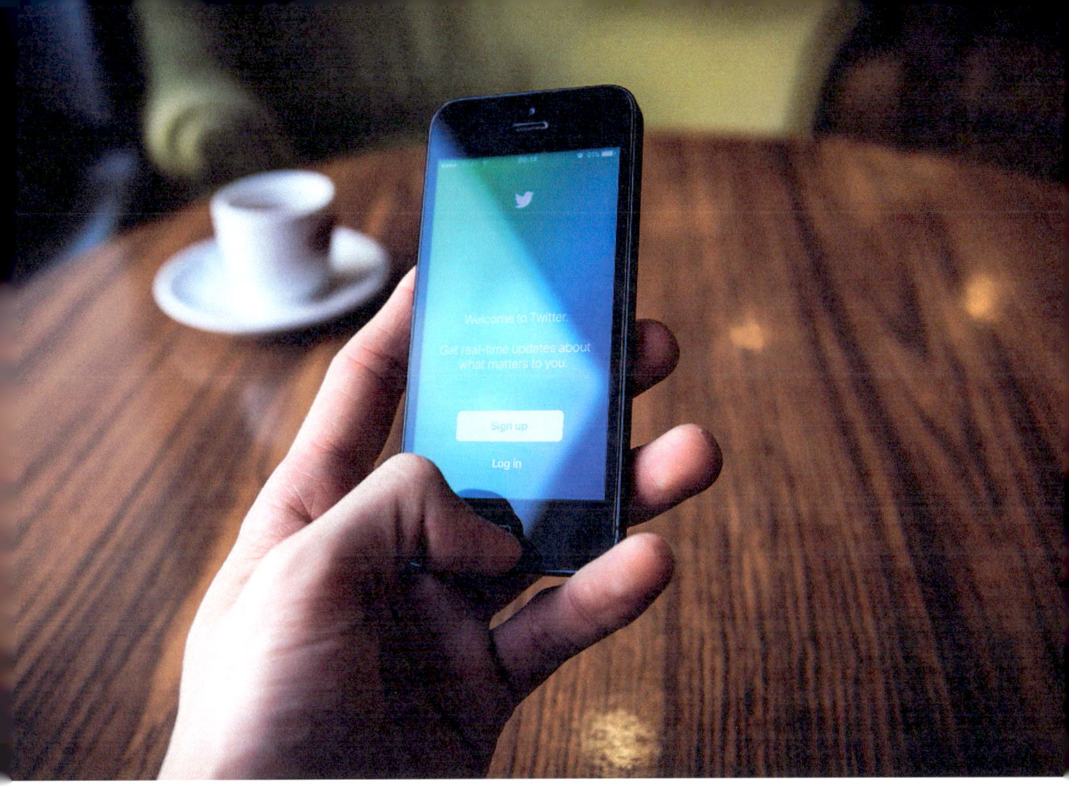

Your business may also need to keep updating content; for instance, if your company has a new product, your followers on social media should be aware as soon as it is launched. Other aspects of your business may suffer as a result of spending too much time on social media. While this can be a challenge, it can be mitigated by hiring experts to handle your social media strategies/efforts while you concentrate on doing what you do best – running your business.

• Diminished Benefits

Your business may fail to realize the benefits of social media marketing if you lack a clear, well-thought-out strategy. You may spend a lot of time or even a good amount of money on creating content, but if you do not have a well-articulated plan, your business will not get the anticipated return on investment Failing to network with your customers or having negative feedback may also result in diminished sales.

2

CHAPTER

STAY AHEAD OF COMPETITION USING SOCIAL MEDIA

Effective Positioning of Your Brand or Small Business on Social Media: Now and the Future

Social media gives brands or small businesses a unique opportunity to extend their reach, build an active online community, and create interactive customer support platforms. However, with the numerous social media networks on the internet today, positioning your brand on

social media and staying ahead of the competition can be a huge challenge for small business owners. Here are effective ways and strategies you can implement to position your brand or small business on social media, now and in the future.

1 Choose the Right Social Media Networks

Sometimes, it is almost impossible to succeed in gaining traction when you spread your tentacles across several social media networks. While it is advisable to create professional profiles on multiple social networks, you need to be cautious to avoid overstretching your resources and capabilities. Remember, not all social media networks will do your small business justice because not all social media networks will align well with your brand's image and goals.

For example, instead of creating a Tumblr profile – a microblogging and social networking website – for your business, consider LinkedIn, where you can interact with other B2B business owners. Some of the major social networks you should consider including in your Social Media Marketing (SMM) campaign include

Facebook, Pinterest, Instagram, Twitter, and LinkedIn. Do extensive research into various demographics (age, sex, location, etc.) of your current and intended markets and determine which social media platforms these demographics use before you choose the most suitable social networks to build your profiles.

2 Define Your Social Media Marketing Goals

Before you start creating and posting content on social media, you should clearly define SMM goals. Some of the primary goals to consider when getting started include:

- brand awareness
- customer engagement
- providing customer service
- lead generation
- driving sales

So, regardless of your goals, ensure that they are clearly defined.

Think of your SMM as you would any other marketing strategy for your brand. In fact, once you identify your goals, it'll be much easier to create your social marketing material. Once you have established your goals, it will be easier to brainstorm effective content ideas and strategies to implement.

3 Post Consistently

Post content on social media accounts and handles regularly to keep them active and ensure your audiences don't forget about your brand. Your followers need to be updated and see your content on their news feeds. In fact, if you realize that your competitors are only posting a handful of times per week, start posting daily to beat the competition and create a lasting impression on your audiences.

Posting frequently reminds your audience that your brand is still thriving and that you are an authority in your niche. Utilize social media

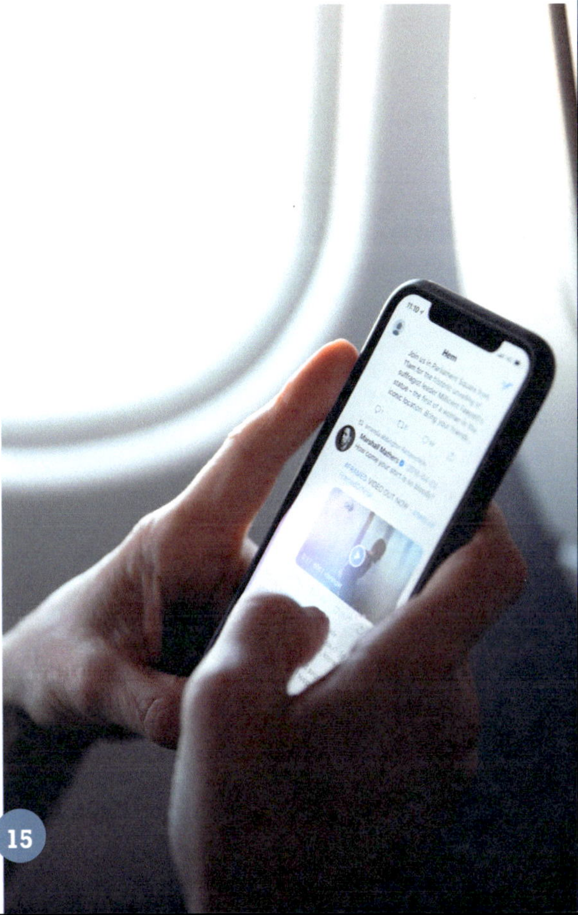

automation tools to help you schedule your posts and automatically post content at predetermined periods. Moreover, consistency in posting useful, engaging content on social media will make your brand appear professional and well-organized.

Make sure you respond to your customers' inquiries, remarks, comments, and complaints promptly through the comment sections or direct messages, depending on the issue being addressed. Being responsive on social media will build a healthy relationship between you and your customers and may prompt them to take action (buy your products or pay for your services!).

4 Give Users a Reason to Follow You

Social media users follow or like certain business pages on social media for different reasons. While others may follow your brand to get more useful content in the future, others may follow you because of a buying intent. Furthermore,

without followers, nobody will see, read, or watch your content. Therefore, you have a responsibility of giving your social media users a reason to follow you.

Once you have a strong social media following, the process of convincing followers to take action becomes much easier and faster. Typically, most online shoppers are more likely to buy from brands they follow or have interacted with on social media platforms. Some great ideas for giving users a reason to follow your brand include: incorporating promotions in some of your posts, creating useful content, offering incentives, and having a customer service representative who manages all social media correspondence promptly.

Positioning your small business strategy on social media will help you make more money from your established customer base, expand your reach, and acquire new customers. Failure to implement an effective strategy that boosts your social proof can be detrimental to your brand or small business. With the proliferation of mobile devices, such as tablets and smartphones, coupled with the growing social media trends, it is essential to have a strong social media presence.

CHAPTER 3

HOW CAN YOU GENERATE MORE TRAFFIC TO YOUR SITE USING **SOCIAL MEDIA?**

Promoting your brand on social media is a reliable, convenient, and effective strategy to generate more traffic to your website. In fact, research shows that social media now drives over 30% of websites referral traffic. Your site can share in these great numbers on a daily basis.

While most businesses and marketers acknowledge this fact, getting started can be overwhelming. So, how can social media help you drive qualified traffic to your website?

The following nine strategies will help you drive more traffic to your website using your social media channels.

1 Share Your Site's URL on Your Profile

First, it's important to create professional, intuitive social media profiles across major social media networks such as Facebook, Twitter, Instagram, LinkedIn, Pinterest, among others.

Secondly, your profiles should have links pointing readers to your website/blog. Your social media profile page provides a perfect opportunity to tell people about your business. Make sure your website address is visible; it should be the first thing people see when they visit your page. This makes the interested readers want to visit the site to see what more they can get from it.

Including a link on your profiles is not only good for SEO but also great for lead generation. This is a viable approach for driving the ideal customer to your website – someone who has already shown interest in your product or service.

A great social media post with a catchy title, description, and visual effects should also have a link to your website. Be sure to share your blog post links

on your social channels. It will enable your viewers to view your posts more often.

Sharing your posts on the various social media platforms will keep the discussion going and get your followers to engage in your posts. You can attract your audience by regularly sharing a variety of posts, including those that are repurposed.

2 Effective Use of Hashtags

Extend your reach and earn more exposure on social media by using hashtags effectively. You should conduct extensive research on trending hashtags related to your niche and employ the best practices of using trending, unique, and succinct hashtags.

The appropriate use of hashtags (relevant and sparingly used) on a social media platform such as Instagram can make your posts go viral quickly and inspire readers to click-through to your website.

3 Make Your Content Shareable

One way of getting more people to read your content is allowing and motivating your followers to share it with their friends.

Ensure that your content is shareable across multiple platforms. You can do this by configuring social media buttons correctly on your website. Unfortunately, some website owners and bloggers fail to confirm whether their content is shareable every time they post new content on their sites. Furthermore, some websites have invisible social media buttons or buttons with broken/ nonexistent links.

Most internet users have short attention spans and won't waste their time struggling to share your content if the social media buttons are not correctly set up.

One advantage of social media is that your followers can easily influence their friends to visit your site once they view something they like. Adding a social sharing tool to your blog builds the trust of your viewers, ultimately increasing your conversion rates.

4 Share Visual Content

Did you know that tweets with images get retweeted more by 150% when they have visuals? This means that if you include visual content in your social media campaigns, you stand a chance to get more traffic to your site.

People tend to share visual content more on social media as compared to other types of content. Make your posts more captivating by adding videos, pictures, infographics, memes, graphs, GIFs, and more. This will spark an interest in your post and motivate your audience to share it.

5 Refer Your Followers to Your Site

Another method of getting your followers to visit your site is by referring them there for information.

Are your fans asking for information that is on your website? Or are they asking about a post that you made some time ago? You can direct them to your site by sharing the links to where the information is on your website.

6 Post When Your Audience Is Most Active

The most appropriate time to post on social media is when your audience activity is at their peak. What's your target audience? What is their online behavior? Are they online to see your post and engage with you? Do your research!

Once you've figured your audience's online activity and when they're most active on each social media platform, you can then tailor your campaigns so that the targeted content is sent to the right audience at the most appropriate time. This way, you will be reaching more leads and increasing your chances to convert some prospects into sales.

Tools such as **Followerwonk** can help you determine when your audience is most active. After getting the information, you should schedule your posts around their activity to increase visibility.

7 Constantly Interact with Your Audience

Constantly interacting with your audience is an effective way to boost traffic to your website and enhance your brand's image and reputation.

Studies have revealed that only 11% of businesses respond to their audiences. By engaging in healthy discussions with your audience, they will be more interested in your business and will want to visit your site to learn more about it. That way, you'll stay ahead of the competition. The result is more sales, a stronger brand image, and increased brand authority.

8 Create Catchy Posts

Instead of posting about the benefits or features of your products all the time, provide value by creating useful and interesting posts that won't bore your audience. Stay relevant to your audience and boost your social proof by posting consistently. However, you have to be careful to avoid being flagged as inappropriate or banned from posting on Facebook groups due to spamming or too much posting.

Instead of posting about the benefits or features of your products all the time, provide value by creating useful and interesting posts that won't bore your audience. Stay relevant to your audience and boost your social proof by posting consistently. However, you have to be careful to avoid being flagged as inappropriate or banned from posting on Facebook groups due to spamming or too much posting.

Consider using social media automation tools such as ***HootSuite, CoSchedule, or Agora Pulse*** to automate the process and let your SMM strategy do its magic in generating traffic to your website.

9 Invest in Social Media Advertising

The number of social media users and the number of business pages keep increasing on a daily basis. This makes it hard for your social media posts to get in front of the desired readers or followers. In fact, an average social media user follows several pages and hundreds of business handles.

Therefore, you need to go an extra mile in order to position yourself strategically and beat your competitors. For example, you can utilize Facebook ads, LinkedIn ads, Twitter ads, and Instagram ads to get more than just organic traffic. Moreover, investing in paid social media advertising will give you more targeted traffic because these paid options allow you to pinpoint and segment your audiences accordingly before launching your ad campaign.

4
CHAPTER

YOUR GUIDE TO GETTING STARTED ON SOCIAL MEDIA

How to Use Social Media for Your Small Business

One of the biggest challenges facing small businesses who are yet to start utilizing the power of social media is the lift-off phase. I am often asked: "How do I start leveraging social media? Where do I even begin?"

We've already seen that social media has the potential of doubling the amount of decent traffic your small business website receives. You need to implement the right social media marketing strategies and utilize the right Social Media Marketing (SMM) automation tools when using social media for your small business.

In order to achieve success and realize an increase in ROI, you have to be consistent and tactical in your approaches. Here are ingenious ways you can use social media to build a loyal online community and stay ahead of the competition.

1 Understand the Benefits of Using Each Network

Innovative small businesses keep discovering new ways of using social media platforms to stay competitive. When getting started, you should understand the benefits of using each of these social media platforms to be more strategic and effective in your SMM approach. Here is a quick rundown of the benefits of using each platform:

- **Facebook:** The platform is regarded as the most used social network, with over 2 billion users and still growing. As a small business owner, you can build your own online community through advertising and storytelling on Facebook. Create a business page and start sharing news content, answering customer questions, and connecting over customer interests.

EXPERT TIPS FOR FACEBOOK BRAND POSITIONING

- Set up and brand your profile.
- Add iFrames to your Facebook Page. This will allow you to place your website, contact form, sign-up form, surveys, blogs, product listings, and campaign landing pages directly on your Facebook page, allowing your fans direct access to these resources.
- Create persuasive CTAs (Calls to Action).
- Post frequently and consistently, at least 4-7 days a week.
- Share photos.
- Share relevant articles.
- Create a fully customized YouTube tab to share videos with your Facebook audience.
- Use paid advertisements, reassess after five days of running the ads, look at the ROI, and determine the next steps.

• **LinkedIn:** This is a great business-oriented platform that brings together potential employers and employees. You can host or join various groups to interact with professionals in your niche and publish articles on relevant topics. Using LinkedIn will help you build a reputation as a thought leader in your industry.

LINKEDIN EXPERT SNIPPETS:

- Set up a well-curated and well-branded LinkedIn company profile.
- Position yourself as a thought leader by writing about your industry.
- Post frequently and consistently, at least 1-5 times per week.
- Use the platform to expand your business contacts.
- Offer credibility by sharing factual information.
- Expand your company network.
- Do extensive keyword research to remain optimized.

- **Instagram and Snapchat:** You can create interesting visual stories using photos and videos about your business and share them on these sites. The platforms have great filter tools for adding visual effects to your messages to make them more animated.

- **Twitter:** You can share brief news, posts, and promotions on this fast-paced networking platform. The site offers you an opportunity to use a Tweet, a micro-message format, to drive traffic to your business site.

EXPERT NUGGETS FOR TWITTER USAGE

- Set up your business profile.

- Adjust your information and bio to improve visibility and to amp your search engine page results.
- Identify key profiles to follow.
- Select best post times. You can use tools such as Timely.Is, Tweriod or Crowdbooster to determine the best times for tweeting when your audience is most active.
- Post frequently, at least 1-8 times per day.
- Curate automated responses to new followers.
- Focus on sending more traffic to your website.
- Position yourself as a thought leader and an expert in your industry by tweeting and retweeting factual and verified information.
- Research and use relevant and existing hashtags to grow your reach.
- Keep expanding your Twitter community by keeping customers and prospects engaged.
- Monitor retweets and mentions.
- Identify and engage influencers and supporters to stamp your brand authority.

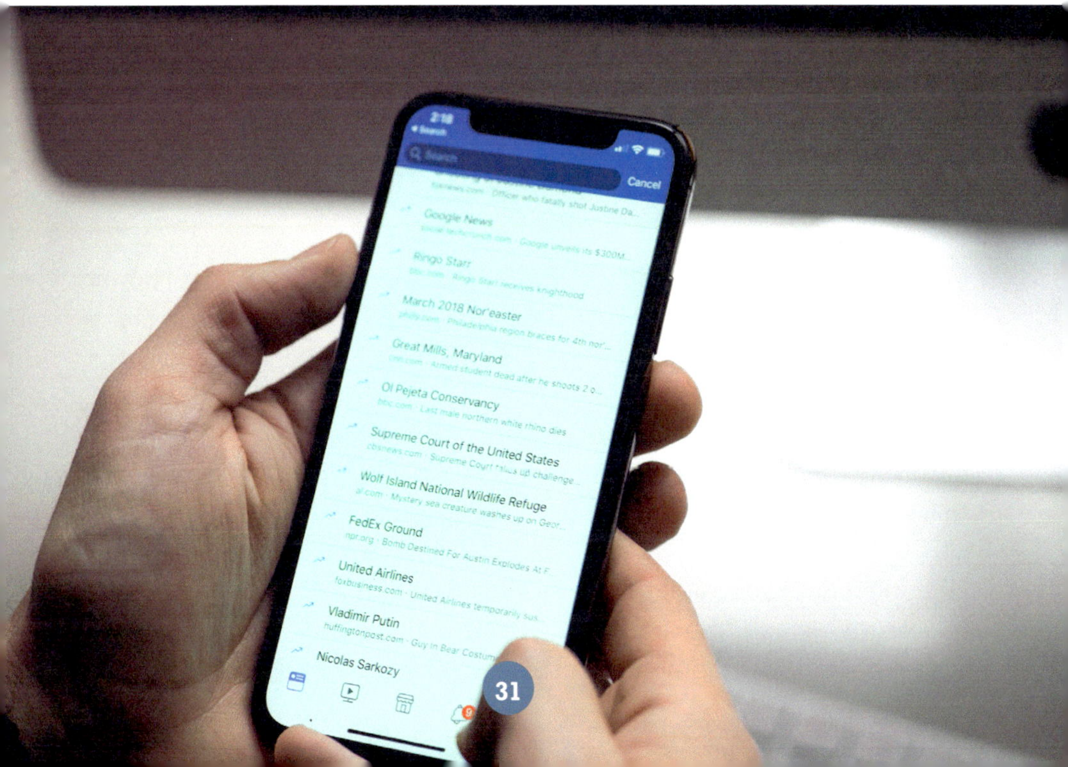

- **Pinterest:** The platform is perfect for sharing themed image galleries. You can promote your business or products and exchange valuable ideas with other contributors in your industry by creating or joining Pinterest boards.

2 Utilize Location-Based Targeting

Use filtering to segment and target a local audience for your small business. In fact, without location-based targeting, social media users who are not interested in your local business or products will be turned off by your posts or ads.

In addition, the filtering feature enables you to utilize your marketing budget optimally. Geotargeting will allow you to show your content or small business to users based on their locations.

Filtering allows you to narrow your audience and find the strongest leads of people interested in your business. When creating your ad campaign, you should start with basic demographics, such as location, age, and income.

3 Create Geotagging Incentives

Geotagging is a great approach when you want to earn clout and boost your social proof. Remember, people can only rely on recommendations from trustworthy sources. The buyer's journey is typically shorter when potential customers are looking for small local businesses as compared to online or multinational enterprises.

Customers will be more willing to act when they come across a positive review with a location tag. Therefore, give your customers an incentive to tag your location when they visit your small business or make a purchase.

4 Track and Measure the Success of Your SMM Campaigns

Without accurate tracking of your SMM campaigns' performances, you might end up wasting your valuable time and resources. You can use social media metrics for monitoring engagement and impressions or analyze the performance using free analytic tools.

With this information, you can tweak your campaigns and pinpoint forms of engagement that trigger the highest conversion rates. This will help you re-adjust accordingly and realign yourself towards the path to success.

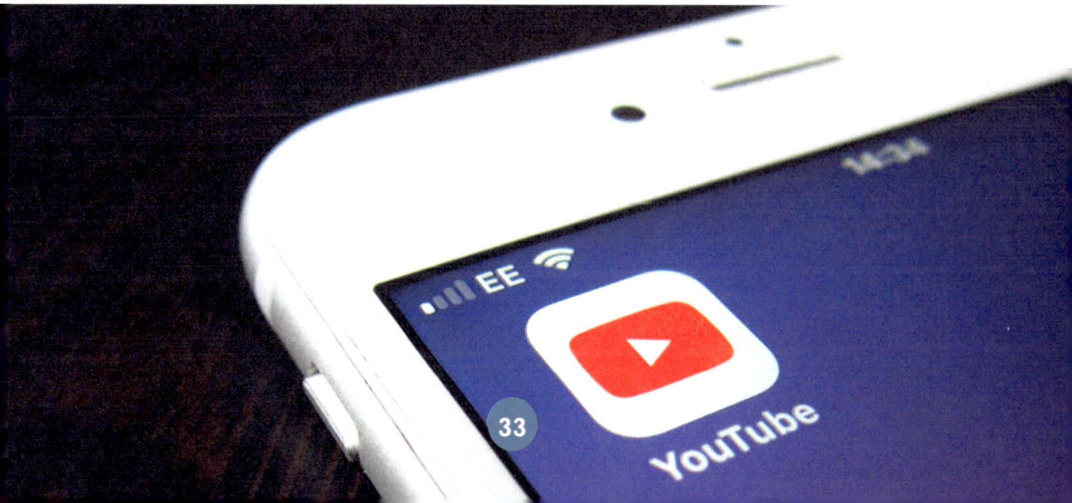

How to Create, Develop, Build and Manage Your Social Media Presence

This section outlines some of the steps that you can use to identify your target audience and implement key messages. The secret is to use different social media channels to position yourself as a leader in your industry, to create a strong network of followers, to share your message and value proposition, and to build a robust overall online presence. By combining these steps and merging them with other strategies discussed throughout the book, you will be able to create a multi-connected stage for information sharing, engagement, and influence.

THINK

This should be the first step when starting or redefining your social media campaign strategy. At this stage, you should clearly articulate:

- What is your company name?
- What's your mission, vision, and target audience?
- What are your messaging persona and tone?

- What is your current market positioning?
- What are your strengths?
- What are your weaknesses?
- Who is your competition?
- What is the competition doing well?
- How will your company/enterprise/brand be better than the competition? What is your unique value proposition?
- What are the roadblocks/barriers/obstacles your organization faces in relation to social media? Time, budget, fear of negative comments?
- How will you benefit from using social media networks?

PLAN

Once you've defined your company and identified your competition, you should then create your social media plan and set your business goals.

- Define your objectives and identify how you plan to achieve them.
- Identify SMART goals. You should be able to measure your performance three months post-launch.
  What are your Facebook, Twitter, LinkedIn, and YouTube goals?

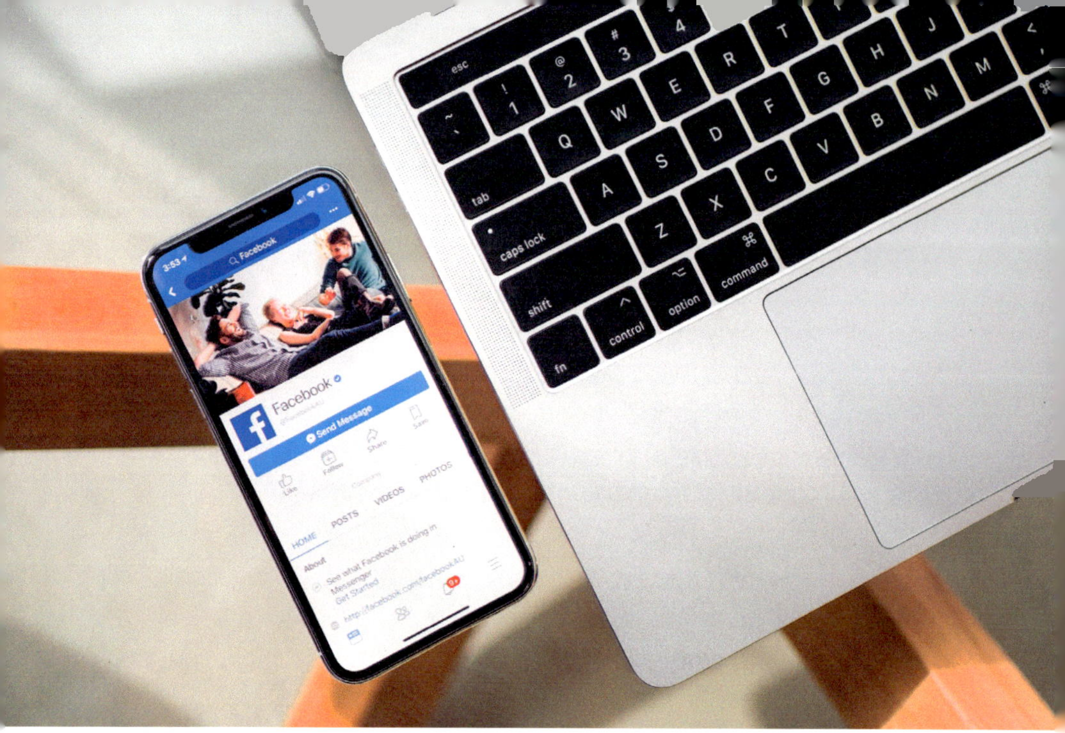

DO

At this point, everything should now be clear, from which social media channels to use and a clear plan for each of them. The next step is to launch and implement/execute your plan! Your goal should be to build a robust fan base of followers and maintain an engaged, strong, and updated online presence throughout all social media channels.

- Identify your target audience
- Promote your brand
- Post about your community
- Share your personality

Here are a few expert tips on how to achieve your goals:

- Create an intuitive visual identity throughout all pages.
- Adjust all information and bios on all channels to improve search and discovery.
- Add themes and details to the content calendar for the year.
- Curate your social media pages to match your brand colors.

- Find bloggers, influencers, and other content creators that you can partner with to grow your brand identity.
- Monitor the conversations. You can do this by using stealth listening tools, such as Hootsuite, TweetReach, PeerIndex, SocialMention, Facebook Insights, or Google Alerts.
- Add your social media addresses to email signatures and all other print media marketing materials.
- Train and encourage staff to posts and mention your brand.
- Ensure consistency in posting on all social media platforms.

EVALUATE

Finally, you should be able to measure and track your metrics.

- Weekly status update. You can measure the impact of the weekly updates through growth in numbers/network, engagement status, influence status, discussions, and mentions.
- The ultimate success criteria should be done after three months. During this time, you should be able to identify whether you've met, exceeded, or fallen short of your goals.

After evaluating your position in relation to your goals, get back to the drawing board and plan on the next course of action. Social media marketing efforts should be consistent and sustained since sometimes they may take time to show results.

5

CHAPTER

ARE YOU READY TO REACH A VAST GLOBAL SOCIAL MEDIA AUDIENCE?

Do you want to deliver your message across multiple cultures and to millions of active communities? This is the right time to get started on social media. Social media is giving small business owners the power to engage new and old clients at a fraction of the cost of traditional marketing. It is allowing social media experts and startups to listen in on market trends and proactively address their customer needs.

After reading this book, you should be able to use social media to market your brand and to get the word out about your small business. Earlier, we saw how you can prepare and curate a robust media strategy that aligns with your business needs. You can choose to use globalized or localized targeting to reach your preferred audience. Let's take a step-by-step recap of what you need to grow your social media traction.

- Establish social media goals that align well with your marketing objectives and business goals.

Please visit my professional website if you'd like my help in achieving your goals:

https://www.paulyniceconsulting.com

To learn more about me and read my other books, please visit

https://www.jeanpaulpaulynice.com.

Take your life to the next level by joining our *living with passion* community of like-minded *purpose-driven* people.

Visit my website https://www.paulyniceconsulting.com and be sure to sign up for my newsletter and follow us on social.

https://www.facebook.com/jeanpaulpaulynice/
https://twitter.com/paulynice
https://www.linkedin.com/in/jnplnce/

Made in the USA
Monee, IL
05 November 2026

67948395R00029